Keys to the Condo
A View of Life by an Almost Old Man

By Danny D. Langone
Photography by Stephanie Natale

PublishAmerica
Baltimore

© 2007 by Danny D. Langone.
All rights reserved. No part of this book may be reproduced, stored in a retrieval system or transmitted in any form or by any means without the prior written permission of the publishers, except by a reviewer who may quote brief passages in a review to be printed in a newspaper, magazine or journal.

First printing

All characters in this book are fictitious, and any resemblance to real persons, living or dead, is coincidental.

At the specific preference of the author, PublishAmerica allowed this work to remain exactly as the author intended, verbatim, without editorial input.

ISBN: 1-4241-7676-X
PUBLISHED BY PUBLISHAMERICA, LLLP
www.publishamerica.com
Baltimore

Printed in the United States of America

Dedication

*To my dad
Alfred M. Langone / USAF
I miss you*

Acknowledgements

My wife Barbara, and family for your love and encouragment

Stephanie Natale for the photos

An Old Gardener's Remorse

Things I did a year ago
Have dropped off by degrees
Like bending over weeding
Now I must do on my knees

Although I must be careful
Where I do that exercise
A post or gate is helpful
If I ever plan to rise

Kneeling down to Mother Earth
A place I loved to be
Has lost its charms immensely
Now I'm way too close to see

Stretching my neck backward
Sighting down my upturned nose
My arthritic finger snatches out
The hazy bright green foes

Rising up with grunts and groans
From that curse I've now been freed
In my hand a new tomato plant
In the ground a smiling weed

Keys to the Condo

As we get older it seems it's our lot
To worry about all the things that YOU'VE got
We watch out our windows and hide by the door
And count all the times that you go to the store

We make it our mission to learn you're routine
Like how many times does your kid slam the screen?
What kind of mail do you have in your box?
When leaving your home do you turn all the locks?

From window to window we watch every move
And judge every action and if we approve
I watch the west side and Gert has the back
Phil has the east side, the fronts up to Jack

We keep a close eye on the things in your trash
If your uncle would die he might leave you some cash
All the bottles and cans in there make it quite clear
If you did get those bucks they'd be gone in a year

We know that you party and we know it's a sign
When your lights are still on"til a quarter past nine
You don't mow your grass on a regular pace
We measure it daily as we pass by your place

You painted the front room we saw through our blinds
The color you chose, it offended our minds
We talked to the neighbors and they would agree
We all felt the same from where each one could see

Thursday is trash day and we say with a prayer
Come Friday we hope your container's not there
But sure as you're born it's still down by the street
And until it's not there, well, our day's not complete

Should we call the police and report all your actions?
Our blood pressure rising with all the distractions
But what if you angered and then moved away?
What in God's name would we do every day?

Black on Black

Black on black and yet I sense you
Lurking stranger in the corner
Your golden eye gives up your stealth
Come closer

Your pinpoint stare cements me to view
Another stranger comes to join
No response, no acknowledgement
Come closer

I cannot clutch stillness as well as you
Anxious tremors beset only my old hands
Your presence is like a hole in the night
Come closer

Aging time melts the bands holding you
Movement without sound of steps
Only my rocking chair creaks in response to your closure
Come closer

Circle of light from my old lamp
A line created over which you will not cross
It reaches out to you but you do not return its warm reflection
Come closer

Your satellite breaks the edge of dawn
Scampering to a waiting gift, he laps the edge of the clotted cream
I sense your transfixed stare upon my gently smiling face, but I
know you won't
Come closer

Condo Nazi

When we moved into the Condo my wife was so relieved
No maintenance and no home repair would plague us she believed
No lawn mowing, no storm windows, no clipping of the hedge
No cleaning out the gutters and no sidewalks must we edge

No vast victory garden harvest with its endless curse of weeds
No cleaning tools and compost piles or sorting last years seeds
No raking leaves in autumn and no shoveling winter's snow
If she ever wants to travel, then we're always free to go

The first week it was wonderful, and I really must admit
To live the life of luxury, why brother, this was it
Rising late in morning became the standard daily fare
Then walking 'round the cul-du-sac a lap or two for air

We were introduced to neighbors and I guess with some surprise
Out of twenty seven condos, in only three of them lived guys
All the rest were owned by widows living off a planned estate
Of some poor departed husband they refer to as their late

I began to wonder briefly contemplating those at hand
If I was just a dinosaur the last in condo land
The last remaining creature of a lost genetic plan
The only one remaining with a worthless prostate gland

If you think for just a moment about the changes in this move
My wife's routine remains the same and does really not improve
Cooking, cleaning, shopping are still on her daily list
While the things I used to do each day are no longer really missed

I've been replaced by someone in a pickup or a van
Who shows up once a week or so since I've been aptly canned
They do the work I used to do on the outside and the lawn
I watch them from the windows, those disgusting low-life spawn

I guess a life as manager will now become my lot
I'll watch them mow the lawn each week and point out every spot
Like a vulture on a fence post I'll survey each handyman
And demean his lack of quality in every way I can

Condo Nazi is a term that now refers to me
Perfection is expected and it better be for free
But deep inside I realize that this person I am not
I just don't know what to do with all the time I've got

So brothers if your wives are now reviewing condo plans
Remember it's a woman's world and not so much a man's
As for me don't worry because next week is looking grand
I get to fix the door knob; it just fell off in my hand

The Retirement Club

Congratulations fella
For turning in your time
You surely need no reason
Last I checked, it weren't no crime

You know we're all behind you
Life of leisure fits us well
And as for your wife's nervousness
I guess only time will tell

Just in case there is a slip up
We have some back-up plans
We found you an old shopping cart
And a bag for aluminum cans

We tried to find you some old boots
Really sorry they don't match
The right ones kinda leaky
But the left one has a patch

My boys down by the river
Asked about your taste in wine
I assured them about your liver
And that Muscatel was fine

Welcome to our retirement club
Your joy I don't wish to rob
But my wife asked me to ask you if
You'd recommend me for your job

For Barbara

Time to look it over
Time to make a plan
Time to spend with family
Time to take a stand

Time to make that appointment
Time to pull a pout
Time to start the oven
Time to take it out

Time to come for supper
Time to pick the beans
Time to put the kids to bed
Time to patch those jeans

Time to say I'm sorry
Time to really share
Time to say I love you
Time to say I care

The Well Bound Book

Glennie failed to rise after ninety-five years
We remember her life like the old pioneers
She wrote a long book that nobody read
I suppose that they would, but it was all in her head

Her mind was a treasure with facts of her time
The whys and the wherefores, the reasons, the rhymes
Who married whom and whose babies died
Which farms had failed and how hard they tried

She used to make soap from old fat and some lye
And knew what to do if it got in your eye
Recalling the years when she had just one dress
And all of love's memories of her husband, Jess

She was good with a thimble, a needle, a thread
Quilts that she made still cover our bed
Her faith never questioned, her eye on the prize
No greater gift given than love from her eyes

To have so much knowledge, it seems such a waste
When we fail to collect it because of our haste
So stop, take a moment with someone of age
Admire their book, let them turn the page

Herman's Little Problem

Herman woke this morning at a quarter after four
It's the same time every morning when his cold feet hit the floor
Navigating through the darkness, grab some underwear that's clean
Throw's the old ones in the hamper sitting near the wash machine

Walking naked to the bathroom, it's not a pretty sight
If Satan saw him coming Scratch would've surely taken flight
Walking past the hall mirror is when it's really sad
He can't remember how many times he thinks he sees his dad

He bolsters up his spirit then moves through the bathroom door
This trip he's made a million times, he hopes a million more
But this time it was different. What was going through his head?
This time he left his glasses on the nightstand by his bed

Casting off this little error feeling no need to correct
He backed up from the mirror so his face he could inspect
He rubbed his hand across his face, a shave he'd surely need
He blindly rummaged through the drawer for a razor to proceed

Finishing his shaving, he must admit was rather rough
His beard had really fought the blade; it had never been that tough
Splashing on some aftershave, this time it really burned
Based on the smell he thought he smelled the product likely turned

Returning to the mirror he attempts to view his hair
What's left up top is thinning but he likes to give it care
The hair cream felt a little thick and seemed to want to smear
But he worked his custom comb over 'til it stretched from ear to ear

The toothpaste tasted funny so he rinsed three times real quick
But then his nose began to run and his tongue felt kind of thick
The aftershave by this time had begun to really stink
So he quickly grabbed some new cologne above the bathroom sink

In his rush he failed to notice as he pried off the new top
The directions clearly stating that you must use just a drop
Three lusty bursts he gave himself and to further his surprise
The stem was pointing backwards and it sprayed him in the eyes

His breath was gone in an instant and his eyes began to swell
In a panic he felt around the drawer, this sting he had to quell
Grabbing a jar of Cold Cream or at least he thought it so
He hurriedly spread it over him from his face down to his toes

The instant coolness greeted him and the emergency seemingly passed
But the emulsion seemed to be changing and the coolness didn't last
In fact it started turning hot and then it really exploded
Especially around his nether world a spot he had foolishly coated

He immediately broke into a dance, his boys going up in a flame
The pain it actually got so bad he completely forgot his name
That's why when a knocking was heard at the door, it was met with no reply
He was struggling to put his tongue in his mouth and open at least one eye

"I moved all your things from your drawer yesterday," called a voice behind the door
"I've put in the things that were on your list that I got at the hardware store"
"I got you some grout for the shower, I hope you wanted clear"
"I got some cream I want you to try to remove all the hair in your ear"

"I got a new brand of drain cleaner and I hope you don't mind that its foam"
"The blue stuff that's there was on special and you use it to soak your comb"
"There is a great big jar of sports cream, I know over time you will use"
"Please change the blade in your razor; I could hardly scrape the mud off your shoes"

On the counter he sat without speaking, nursing his swollen pride
Shaking his head very slowly, he silently sniffed while he cried
Where had he gone wrong so long ago, had he married the missing link?
He shouldered the blame for his error as his hair slowly fell in the sink

Danny's Dungarees

I have an old pair of dungarees
I like to just call them bibs
The knees are both out and the seat kind of pouts
But they really fit my jib

My wife, she says they are awful
A point that is hard to deny
But comfort's the point when I stroll 'round my joint
And acceptance is something she'll try

As long as I stay in the garden
Don't go wandering around in the street
Don't stand by the door, don't go to the store
And hide from the neighbors we meet

I've done all she has asked, but I'm worried
Seems rumors in mass do abound
Neighbors saying aghast that I've suddenly passed
And I'm now six feet under the ground

I suppose I should give up this fashion
And return from the land of the dead
Just give back the rice, the spaghetti was nice
But boy was I wonderfully fed

Moses Remembered

I lost my friend in March last year
His memory haunts me still
The softness of his eyes so clear
The power of his will

We walked together on a path
The direction seldom varied
No rush to end or misplaced wrath
When one of us had tarried

He'd meet me every morning
With the same sweet smiling face
It never seemed to bother him
When I stomped around the place

His patience everlasting
He would silently abide
When I stopped my errant casting
He would slide up to my side

His look filled me with calm
His concern for me so true
He applied his hidden balm
And my spirit was renewed

I no longer walk the path with him
Pain and suffering prevailed
But I held his head as his breath grew slim
And his heartbeat slowly failed

I know had I been the first to go
He would have mourned the same for me
Now I walk the path unvaried slow
With the pain from which he's free

Savoy

I went to hear a big band play on Sunday afternoon
Glenn Miller hits
Cab Calloway fits
And all the forties tunes

The orchestra assembled with their instruments in tow
Saxophones
Gold Trombones
Trumpets filled the row

Youth was not a term I'd use to identify the crowd
Hands in knots
Liver spots
Shoulders arthritis bowed

But most were not put off by age as they dressed up to the nines
Jewels and curls
Dresses that swirl
Gentlemen standing the line

I watched as they shuffled to the dance floor
Grasping at chairs
Feet guiding stares
A few seemed hardly up to the chore

Forming up into couples as the music began to play
Box stepping feet
Fox trotting beat
You could see all the age slip away

I mused as they circled, what a change to the scene
Smiling faces
Warm embraces
The dancers had returned to the age of nineteen

The lesson not lost, all were given a chance
Lose the ages
Turn back pages
I turned to my wife, would she like to dance?

Ascension in Decline

Birth
Ascending into life
Center of the Universe
Youth experimenting with fire
New experiences from old memories
Young adult tampering with the seeds of life
Too fertile ground robs some of their childhood
Adulthood don the ornaments of responsibility
Some will crush under the weight of ambition
Middle-aged softness with strong desires
Hiding the scars of disappointment
Old age wrapped in cotton dreams
Returning to the past
Spiraling down
Death

Keppa's Confusion

Stay to the right
Nice people don't fight
Clean up your room
Eat with a spoon

That's too much to drink
Put your dish in the sink
Did you do your chores?
Going out? Close the doors

Who taught you to dress?
Don't make a mess
Watch what you say
Don't act that way

Sit up, sit straight
You can't go, it's too late
Your hair needs a comb
Don't go off alone

Sit down in your seat
Did you wash your feet?
Hold the rail on the stair
Don't lean back in your chair

Hold down your voice
You don't get a choice
Are they talking to me?
or my grandchild of three?

Diner Don Juan

I was sitting at the restaurant
For my morning waste of time
Catching up on local gossip
Senior coffee's just a dime

Waitress ain't bad looking
My order each day is the same
I kinda think she likes me
She calls me by my name

I try to talk real witty
If she's standing near ear shot
I look for her reaction
Perhaps she'll think I'm hot

Peering down the counter
Sizing up the other men
I add up the competition
With a number one to ten

Today they're a bunch of zeros
Have to say I'm feeling great
After all, I'm quite conservative
I rate myself an eight

Taking one more look around
I'm suddenly taken aback
When I see her sitting in a booth
My love train jumps the track

The guy she's with is laughing
As she whispers in his ear
I feel my chances slipping
Blow my nose to staunch a tear

I knew our love was over
When she missed my sixth refill
So I pulled myself together
And I went to pay the bill

On the way to the register
I had an epiphany
To get a second chance
A big spender she'd need to see

So when she rang the order up
I didn't think it strange
To see the look upon her face
When I told her keep the change

I can hardly wait 'til tomorrow
I'll be back at the same old time
And find out how she spent the whole
Quarter and a dime

Motivation

Why must aging haunt me? Almost daily now it seems
In the mirror after rising, during all my day's routines
At evening when the stillness often causes me to slow
Taking stock of where I've been and how much further I must go.

I worry that my ending will leave a cluttered scene
Dues unpaid for dreams unborn or chasing harebrained schemes
A calling perhaps is what it means or a crisis at middle age
But I cannot rest until my views are put down on a page

So here are the workings of my mind spelled out in poems and prose
I hope that some will make you think and others tweak your nose
I have no incite into destiny and my story's not all told
It's just a view of a thing or two from a man that's almost old

Lexapro

My mind is like a movie house
Work is the featured show
It starts the moment I close my eyes
I have only ten reels to go

The opening starts with misgiving
And problems start flickering past
The bad ones are usually in color
With a quite lengthy list of the cast

The projector searches for focus
The sound man turns down the roar
I twist in my seat, look for something to eat
Then I'm startled awake with a snore

Fire and Ice Revisited

Once I read a poem debating
Would the end be fire or ice?
I remember then relating
That neither one was nice

The options seemed so limited
Could it be so black or white?
Could the end be something else instead?
From a factor quite contrite

Man's ego is the sword he thrusts
His mind serves as his shield
His creative dominance he trusts
Will make all nature yield

But Mother Nature chuckles
As we terrorize the land
And she'll simply slap our knuckles
When we get so out of hand

She'll do it with a puzzle
From pieces we create
Like a dog who wears a muzzle
We'll begin to salivate

The answer will evade our reach
We'll work it day and night
But eventually we hit a breach
And lose our futile fight

Then nature picks up on her course
Continuing her plan
As if there had not been a force
The era known as man

Queen for a Day

My little grandson Joey
Asked what he'd be on Halloween
Responded quite distinctly
He would like to be a queen

Once his parents stopped their laughing
And the scene had settled down
They both were taken back
By Joey's great big frown

They tried to appease him
Perhaps a better choice
But Joey was tenacious
Tears were stifling his voice

I remember thinking thankfully
That my dad was no longer here
He'd had a fit about a kitchen set
Santa almost brought one year

When the big day finally happened
His mom had dressed him as a fly
And he left for school unhappy
But at least he didn't cry

That night at home watching TV
A commercial caught his glance
And once it was completed
He began to sing and dance

Oh I am the Queen Lumestra
I'm the fairest in the land
Well what do you do with a dancing fly?
Just give the boy a hand

At five you're filled with imagination
But fortunes can be lost as you age
As for now Joey is the Queen Lumestra
Until life catches up and flips the page

Rhythm Rocking

Rock and dream
Rock and dream
Life is like a flowing stream

Rock and dream
Rock and dream
Try and reclaim my self-esteem

Rock and dream
Rock and dream
Watch all my wishes go up in steam

Rock and dream
Rock and dream
What's it all supposed to mean

Tick Tock
Tick Tock
Rock and dream 'til the end of life's clock

Take No Prisoners

I'm a prisoner in a body that does not belong to me
I should really know because I've been aware of it since three
My original was tender, stretched with ease, and rather plump
And my mother used to tease me about the dimples on my rump

My suspicions started growing when I crowded fifty-five
When I found I couldn't turn my neck when backing down my drive
Then at sixty years this thing I'm in refused to bend and stoop
At sixty-five the grip took hold and it couldn't take a poop

The walnut that it's sitting on can really make me moan
It no longer needs my earmuffs as it seems to grow its own
Its knees are sagging badly and its legs are way too thin
But it seems to make it up with its belly and its chin

The skin, it has a brown spot that I thought resembled Maine
But this year it seemed to grow quite large and now it looks like Spain
Its eyes are really baggy and its hair is really thin
This is not the real container that I first was fitted in

I'm sure I am a victim of some midnight UFO
That took my real body as a joke some years ago
If an alien is reading this I would anticipate
You can have it back, I'll be in the sack and asleep, I'm sure, by eight

The Gift

A discarded shoebox covered with crinkled aluminum foil
Red velvet ribbon held precariously with scotch tape
The boy admires its beauty
Satisfied

Lights from a thousand Christmas trees dance off the box
Held firmly in his lap during the long car ride
The boy is too small to see out
Magical

Warm greetings and familiar voices upon the arrival
Steaming flavors draw them in
The boy will not take off his coat
Anxious

Authority relenting, released into the night to follow a snow filled path
Warm breath frosts the silver treasure
The boy scurries
Anticipating

Stark white house with darkened windows, locked doors stuck shut, unused
A tiny light above a dissolving side porch
The boy knocks with mittened hand
Concerned

Door opening, admittance granted, retreating to a cot by the kitchen wall
Frail gray flesh as thin as the film over the octogenarian's eyes
The boy breathes in the smoky wood heat
Relieved

Renewing friendship, acts of kindness, loneliness chased to the corner of the room
The old man embraces two gifts
The boy sits watching as tear drops wet a yellowing pillowcase
Rewarded

Kappa's Garden

Tommy has a baseball card
Kimmy has a crayon
Barbara has an apple
And a counter they could play on

Toby had white curly hair
Kippy had a house
Moses had the softest eyes
Grady has a mouse

Evan likes to play with cars
Lexy likes to read
Jenny has the cutest face
Halley likes to lead

Robert works crosswords in ink
Mary loves the Cross
Donna has a pup named Tyke
We're not sure who's the boss

Joey's love is numbers
Claire loves fancy shoes
Cuthbert wanders round the house
With a ball he often chews

And I sit in the garden shed
An old pipe set to light
Fondly thinking of them all
While rocking in the night

WHEN?

When our eyes grow too dim and our ears don't react
When we no longer trust in our digestive tract
When we still feel a chill in the mid summer heat
When our teeth are so short we no longer eat meat

When a swaggering walk means our knees have gone bad
When referring to our doctor we call him young lad
When our skin has more spots than a Dalmatian pup
When we're given a drink in a pink tippy cup

When half of a sandwich is all we can eat
When a nap at 10:30 is considered a treat
When dinners at four and bedtimes at eight
When a cup full of water is holding our plate

When our navel's a marker where our waist used to be
When we sleep for four hours but need more than one pee
When a hot looking woman has only two chins
When the priest falls asleep when reviewing our sins

When reading the paper is a day that's well spent
When drinking one beer is enough to get bent
When we fart as we walk and nobody cares
When three steps is considered a full flight of stairs

When reading this list feels like it's too close to home
A biography written and not just a poem
When we wonder just when this attack really ends
Just stop all your bitching, pull up your Depends

Winter's Secret Garden

Cat tracks down the garden path
Destination is unsealed
In summer time its presence
Would never be revealed

By the corner of the shed
A mouse has built his little room
But the cat tracks make me wonder
If perhaps this was his tomb

The goldfish in the pond
By the heater they repose
Dreaming of the warmer days
And the fountain when it flows

Under the bird feeders
Peppered snow; seed gone to waste
Cast out by the sparrows
With their picky sense of taste

Waste not, wants not lessons
Are not lost on squirrels and dove
As they relish in the harvest
Of the manna from above

A hawk's wings perfect image
I see clearly as I go
Like an angel come from heaven
Who had tapped upon the snow

Sculptures from the bones of plants
With skin of snow and ice
Gives meaning to their passing
With autumn's sacrifice

Winter's secret garden
Perfection to the eye
I could never match its beauty
No matter how I try

Sparks

Yellow leaves rising up with the wind
Leaping to the ground below
Life ends

Two children dangling their feet in a stream
One runs off to follow a floating leaf
A friendship ends

Stillness
Snap
I remember how tears flow

Father and Mother
Warm and fed
God mind is born into the world

The child stumbles and cries
No one stops
A man arises unaware

One dish on the table
No mail in the box
But no one is alone, death is waiting patiently

Breath of Life
Flame of Hope
The candle of man consumes them without regard

Eating sweet raspberries
Seeds stuck in my teeth, I keep eating
The lasting marriage

Red Jelly bean
Green Jelly Bean
Prejudice raises its head

Galaxies swirling in space
Blazing with a million stars
Strike another match

The edge of space
Unreachable because of man's own invention
I reset my watch

Reaching with his arm
Reaching with his mind
Both ends of the string are the same

In order to live
Something must die
The butcher puts his thumb on the scale

A child plays marbles in the park
Scratching a circle in the sand
The planet adjusts itself

Fresh spring rain
Washes the dust from the path
A dog rolls on an earthworm

An old man sitting on a bench
His mind in yesterday
I close the closet door and he is gone

Hills and valleys
Rivers running deep
I turn my wet face from the mirror

Beautiful trees
Branches reaching to the heavens
I push the dust from a neglected bookcase

The aging dowager powders her face
The scars of age hiding under the whiteness
Winter returns

The child runs off gleefully chanting
Grandpa slips the key back into his pocket
Life's lesson lost

The knife disemboweled it
Redness oozing and seeping
Ice cream would be nice

Two dogs fighting over a bone
The graveyard watches
Indifferent

Dogs beaten and starved
Slinking back to the man
Buy another gold tooth

Pump a shell into the chamber
Counting the rounds as you pull the trigger
Happy Birthday

Religion's Reality

To earth I came and for millions of years
I prospered here through many tears
But DNA that created me
Will soon be loosed and trouble free

Viruses will my carriage be
Trailing through oceans and over seas
Lifting up on windy lace
Distributed outward into space

And after a millennial time
Without reason, without rhyme
I'll settle down in a distant place
And regenerate the human race

I will not remember my mortal name
Or the beautiful rock from whence I came
I will forget life's lessons long
My lover's scent, my mother's song

But when awareness of my soul
Retakes myself and some selfish goal
Invades my mind I vainly hope
I'll recall enough to truly cope

And when in anguish I look to the sky
Call out God's name and ask him why
A faint remembrance I hope there will be
And realize that God is ME.

Danny's Dilemma

I cannot work for that old man
My mind rejects his business plan
I stand amazed that he's gotten so far
His office staff, His brand new car

I'm sure I beat his intellect
A chink in his armor I surely detect
It's amazing that no one but me is aware
The rest are so stupid or don't really care

So off on my own I deliberately fly
All that I need is desire to try
The American dream unencumbered by lot
Just grab it and run, make my break, take my shot

Well maybe some tools and a space would be nice
There are so many people with willing advice
But when I talk money, they all disappear
Or act like they're stricken with wax in their ear

I won't listen to people who don't know the way
Although they all claim to have been in the fray
I won't be deterred by their lack of foresight
My horoscope says I've a gift and it's right

A few hundred dollars is all it will take
Would they dare to say no, won't they see their mistake?
They'll all kiss my feet I say with a sneer
When I become rich, I predict in a year

The banker's ineptness was glaringly clear
If I had what he wanted would I even be here?
His insulting demeanor, Is he pulling my leg?
Just wait 'til I'm rich and he'll come down a peg

With darkness descending I rifled the car
Three pennies, a lozenge, and a dried out cigar
My future was fading, could this be the end?
Should I just give it up and stop bucking the trend?

I have always been someone who fought the word," no"
The word simply means find a new way to go
If I can't move forward then I must learn to stall
So I simply took Peter's so I could pay Paul

The house payment lightened by half did the trick
If my wife would have known she would surely be sick
Why should she worry with this little hitch?
But it's best not to tell her until we are rich

Five years have past since that fateful event
I only need five hundred more for the rent
The space is too small and a move is made clear
Surely this means there'll be riches next year

Ten years and counting and another new space
And now there are people all over the place
The State was elated when they gave me the bill
I hope it's the last year I crawl up this hill

Paying the workers as they pass by my door
My wife wonders if she can go to the store
I want to say yes but the checks have been sent
And I still need three grand just to meet this months rent

The years have passed twenty, my hair's all turned gray
I wonder if business is really this way
Illusions of grandeur that pass with the years
You measure success by the depth of your tears

My heads in a daze as I walk down the hall
This harness I'll wear 'til the day that I fall
Then suddenly voices come at me quite clear
A message for someone not meant for my ear

The old mans a joker and he don't have a clue
If I owned this place I know what I would do
A few hundred dollars is all it would take
In a year I'd have plenty and a house on the lake

It's amazing how circles in life seem to run
The pride that we lose with reality's stun
I don't say a thing as I sit in my car
With three pennies, a lozenge, and a dried out cigar

Discouragement

Winter is here in crusty patches
Pinching, contracting, scarring, distracting
Holding fast old rusty latches
Shivering, slipping, temperatures dipping

Moods are dark to match the days
Short, curt, brisk, quick spurt
Fashion retreats from colors to grays
Long flannel skirt, old woolen shirt

The animals know it's a time for retreating
Fox to the den, roost for the hen
A look from the cat is its only greeting
I'll write when I can, ink's froze in the pen

Deep Dish Doctor

When I got up this morning, my left finger had a pain
I thought hard all about it could it be somehow a sprain?
I don't remember anything that would end with that result
So I gave my doctor one quick call to possibly consult

The automatic message system answered the third ring
By this time my left digit had begun to really sting
To speak in English would I like to push the number one
So I did and then a click, and then a dial tone I was done

I redialed almost instantly I was a little mad
To have to talk to a machine it makes me kind of sad
This time before it finished I hit the number two
And was greeted by dead air space and again the call was through

Yelling at the phone to a phantom person who's not there
I insult the phone and all the people dealing with its care
The third time turned the trick and I finally heard a voice
"Tony's Pizza, Is this delivery or pickup what's yer choice?

After a moments silence almost desperate on my knees
I order one large pizza, pepperoni hold the cheese
I figure that I'll show the kid my finger when he's here
Cuz a house call from a doctor ain't been made in forty years

Pipe Dreams

When I was growing up the rage was everybody smoked
Then in the sixties era all the hippies liked to toke
I held off smoking cigs until my graduation night
Then I fired one up and smoked two packs probably for spite

I thought it was a sign that I had finally come of age
Adulthood swept upon me having turned the childhood page
My girlfriend at the time gave me an ashtray and a pipe
What an image it projected, man, I bought into the hype

Thirty years I huffed and puffed, three packs a day was it
I would have made it four a day but my budget wouldn't fit
Smoking was a habit that I did quite unaware
It was also something you could do and no one seemed to care

One day a thought came to me that perhaps I'd better quit
While I sat blue faced and gasping with my morning coughing fit
Stopping wasn't difficult but staying stopped was rough
For ten years I put up a fight each day was really tough

After all the years, I've slipped back to smoking my old pipe
The insurers and the lawyers and the government all gripe
Those guys are really happy that tobacco has us hooked
Just sit back for a moment and let's take another look

The government embraces it like liquor, oil, and now
Either party can hide behind our health while milking this cash cow
With righteous indignation they can safely take these stands
While raking in new taxes most to use for other plans

The insurer's cry because huge profits now they may not make
Science having stretched our lives, new odds they'll have to take
The chance that smoking may in fact lead to a lingering fate
They can up the score if they pay out more than their factors calculate

Class actions by attorneys in this litigious world today
Are nothing more than one big score for the firm on its payday
The victims hardly profit from the courtroom's big charade
The amount they get if any pales compared to what was made

I'm not defending smoking and I think it still is bad
But I see us all as victims that continually are had
Public good as a reason is really just a ghost
For profit is the motive by those we trust the most

Pariah

Desperation no longer haunts me since I've mellowed over years
I no longer get so anxious that I break down into tears
I don't know if I've just hardened like a cheese rind in the air
Or if possible the end result holds nothing for which I care

It seems that I have spent my life in a state of constant wait
For something to arrive or go to change my envisioned fate
A victim of the media and societies constant rub
Has calloused my emotions, worn my pencil to a stub

I no longer worry endlessly about the impressions that I make
Or my credit rating number, or if my membership they'll take
I don't want plastic cards, neither platinum nor gold
To think you have to have them is a value over sold

The ruler that is used today to measure your success
Is highly over rated and contributes to the mess
The planning and the scheming of some phantom face unknown
Who holds your key to happiness a decision not your own

I reject his intrusion and his meddling in my life
This man made apparition who creates a world of strife
This pariah with its grasp around our imagined state of need
Feeding well upon us daily and encouraging our greed

A Gulp of Golf

On a pleasant cold fall morning long before the birds awake
We assembled in our fashion on a golf course by a lake
It had always been our habit to attend with groggy cheer
To be honest there were some of us who golfed just twice a year

The leader of this dawn event might seem a bit out spoken
So we named the day out of respect," The Garstecki Polish Open"
Most of us were duffers, a little pleasure we would seek
While others sold insurance and could golf six times a week

The teams were selected by a drawing of some cards
Garstecki shuffled them under a close watch from some guards
It's not that he would cheat and fix some teams that can't be beat
But he's known to bend to pressure from some rivalry in heat

The teams were now assembled and it was time for our first drink
If golf was all you thought we did, better have a second think
Beer and a Bloody Mary were the selected bill of fare
While cigarette and cigar smoke in an instant filled the air

By the time we got into our carts to head off to the tee
We all had had at least one drink and some of us had three
By the time we're at our starting points it's not so odd to see
Three of four guys searching for a place where they could take a pee

In preparation stretching is important we all know
But honestly I tell you most of us can't touch our toes
So we do a little windmill with the club behind our back
And we swing the driver back and forth, an imaginary whack

The first one up to hit is just a sacrificial lamb
If he duffs it as expected he'll receive a cat call slam
But if by chance he hits it, even though his eyes are closed
He's labeled "you da man" and hears a lot of "way to goes"

The first hole passes normally our heads still in the game
The second hole is somewhat off but the result is still the same
But by the third hole you can sense that there's a certain type of change
When the group behind you shells you with their balls when you're in range

The voices all grow louder and the language is quite blue
It's perhaps because we all have had another drink or two
I've noticed that the group ahead has had some long delay
One guy walked off to take a leak and forgot he was here to play

The drink cart buzzed the course, a postman on appointed rounds
She had to fill up twice to make it once around the grounds
Her job was not as easy as we all would like to think
Dodging errant golf balls hit by men whose golf game really stinks

Things eroded badly as each team approached the turn
A whole team came up missing and there rose up some concern
They were finally located in a bar just down the road
They were too drunk to continue and their carts had to be towed

Another fellow on a team of veterans so I'm told
Was sent home prematurely because his shoes began to mold
It seems he dropped his cigar in the outhouse on hole ten
Then slipped off of the seat when trying to get it back again

The remaining teams continued although I really don't know why
When you asked them how they're doing you were sure to hear a lie
The response that they're ten under was an incriminating clue
When you know the best they've ever done was over par by two

What do you expect from someone in a Hawaiian shirt and shorts?
Especially when it's forty-five in the weather man reports
It's no wonder that when teeing off there's stiffness to their swing
Thank goodness for the booze they drank cuz they don't feel a thing

The ugliness continues when you watch how some guys play
In a somewhat hazy stupor they appear to take all day
First they measure out the distance and proceed to take their stance
Then they stand for twenty minutes like they're stuck there in a trance

One fellow that I watched and I'll resist from saying who
Takes untold time to pick a club then usually chooses two
Advancing on the ball he takes six practice swings with each
Then hits the ball, if at all, just slightly out of reach

Then there's the guy who lets it fly to the left and then the right
If we let him search for his lost balls we'd be there half the night
It's best to let him play out the first ball he comes across
For as many balls as he seeds the course, he can't afford the loss

When at last they all make it back to the clubhouse before dusk
They all are pretty boisterous and they smell like groundhog musk
The stories that they tell about their golf game often pales
To the score they post, like minnows that with time turn into whales

Eventually they all drift home, some linger more than most
Reluctant to bring closure to the Open and its host
But they shouldn't worry too much for their phones will surely ring
As all BS is welcome at the Do Not Open in the spring

After weeks of recuperating and their heads begin to clear
Speculation starts to fly as to how they'll do next year
To blame it all on drinking well it wasn't really fair
If truth be known, they claim it was the freshness of the air

That really doesn't help explain the golf cart in the pond
Or the fact I can't find half my clubs of which I'm really fond
I vaguely do remember what a fun time we had there
When Patrick wore that sod as a replacement for his hair

I hope that in your life you have the chance to just let loose
At least one day every year you can escape the business noose
If you have the chance to try it I suggest you just take off
And refresh your thirst for freedom with a great big gulp of golf

Cat Chat

I own a cat named Grady, I guess that's not completely true
Because a difference of opinion exists between us two
The subject most objected too pertains to ownership
When he hears me say I "own "him well it's just a verbal slip

He prefers to believe he "allows" me to provide for his whims each day
And "allows" me to sometimes pet him, which he considers sufficient pay
He "expects" that I surrender his favorite spot on the bed
Or when he gets cold in the nighttime, he "consents" to sleep on my head

He's "indignant" when I continue sleeping when he "insists" that I open the door
When he feels his passions rising to go out at a quarter past four
He's "displeased" when I start my complaining while he sits on the threshold in doubt
He's "upset" with my lack of true patience while he decides if he's inside or out

God forbid that I tell him to hold it or perhaps consider using the box
If I close the door before he's decided he'll tear a big hole in my socks
Regardless of what "I've" decided if he feels the box will not do
He'll wait til I'm soundly asleep and then quietly pee in my shoe

With the morning comes all the yelling and my rage after finding the prize
He simply rolls over and forgives me for making him open his eyes
They say that a dog loves to be owned by a master of whom he adores
But a man to a cat is a servant to cater to him and do chores

Chocolate Gorgonzola

Born to be an Angel Cake that's what I thought I'd be
A fate cast upon me since I left the bakery
I always thought success would bring a frosting judged the best
And sprinkles and some cherries for a crown in which I'd dress

A creation like no other, a baking wonder sought by all
They would push me up the ladder and expect I take the call
But I didn't realize the time and the temperature it would take
So the end was disappointing, the result a half baked cake

I was crusty on the outside but on the inside I was goop
Instead of slicing thinly you might have to use a scoop
It was too late to replace the lid and heat me one more time
Could life's cherry bowl be filled with sour lemons and a lime?

I dragged my doughy stature around each diner, plate to plate
But mostly they would pick at me, an unappetizing trait
No one seemed to want to take the risk to take a bite
Most of the time I sat out on the counter over night

I don't know why exactly but I was never thrown away
I sat out on that counter for almost sixty years today
I look a little moldy and I've got a skin like rind
But I have to tell you honestly, I'm a one and only kind

Today I found a fellow looking at me with bright eyes
He poked me in the stomach; we were both a bit surprised
Then he cut me open gently, took a piece of me with ease
That's when I realized I was really a big cheese

Dancing the Two Step

Waking up this morning I had an overwhelming dread
Something in my mind kept warning," Dan, go back to bed"
But I sloughed it off as meaningless and got up anyway
That was number one, my first mistake to start the day

When ever I make a mistake as I'm often known to do
I know it won't be long before there's screw up number two
I sneak around just waiting for the other shoe to drop
It's a natural progression, an event that I can't stop

I get to work unhampered; it's a miracle to me
Surely two will hit me before I leave the place at three
Skulking rather quietly, fly below the radar screen
I hang in there 'til lunch, closed office door so I'm not seen

I head out to lunch alone because a witness I don't need
If number two should strike me, all precautions I must heed
I only have a salad and an apple for my lunch
I really want much more but that might be the second crunch

I walk back to the office because I dare not take the car
I should walk more often as it's really not that far
Thinking it's a shame to have to waste such a fine day
To have it ruined just because number two is on the way

Sequestered in my office I pull down the window shade
It's angering to lose the day 'cuz of the first mistake I made
I figure that's the reason that I'm having a great day
When 'ol two finally happens it's twice as bad that way

It was just short of a miracle that I got home from work
Nothing happened to me which I'm sure was just a quirk
It must be going to happen during dinner or TV
"Ol number two was coming I'll just have to wait and see

Wonder of wonders I'm just about in bed
Nothing has happened; my mind was filled with dread
Wasting the whole day in anticipation of 'ol two
Was that the actual mistake, the dropping second shoe?

Rx

Sometime when life is beating you down
And nothing is going your way
It's best to just try to stop thinking
For a second or two through the day

Take a deep breath and then exhale
Releasing your stress as you blow
Allow all the feelings to follow
And just for a moment they'll go

The stress is from constantly waiting
Either for something good or for bad
Debating the course to be taken
Even though there's no choice to be had

The answer may not be what we're wanting
Pending changes unwelcome at best
It will surface when it's truly ready
No matter how we beat our chest

Defeating your stress is dependent
Not on how much resistance you show
But your skill at accepting what will be
And your strength at just letting it go

Sealed Away

I know you're there behind the closet door
Each time I open it I can smell your essence
Memory turning pungent from the dark
Cherished adornments imprisoned in idle wait

Others would have me cast you out
Release the only bond with which we are still joined
I have no need to move beyond this moment
I will lock you safe away, untouched except by me

I know you're walking just beyond my view
And I will someday be released to follow your path
Memories' scent may be all I'll have to find you
When I'm blinded by the light from the other side

For now I'll close the door, please forgive me
End our visit for the day, but I'll return
Unless answers to my prayers are finally granted
And the gift to walk beside you I have earned

Senior Discount

I don't know how it happened
And I still don't have a hunch
I had gone into a restaurant
To treat my dad to lunch

After ordering, my father
Who wasn't anybody's fool
Asked for a senior discount
Which he does now as a rule

The little waitress looking
First at him and then at me
Smiled sweetly and responded
That both our drinks were free

I remember thinking darkly
That her ability to gauge
The difference twixt my dad and I
Was due to her young age

Oh sure I have some graying hair
And my middles rather plump
And the reading glasses on my face
Tend to make me look a frump

But Hey I think it's obvious
That I'm no elder sage
I'm sure they'd use my picture
When discussing middle-age

My father asked me frankly
When I complained about the sting
Why was it that I took the drink
And never said a thing?

Returning home discouraged
Feeling ready for a nap
My wife inquired about my day
I snarled that it was crap

She handed me a letter
And my glasses so I could see
The bold imprinted writing
From the group A.A.R.P.

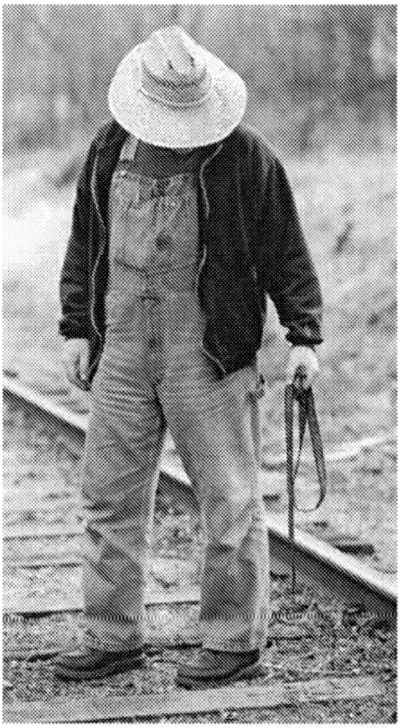
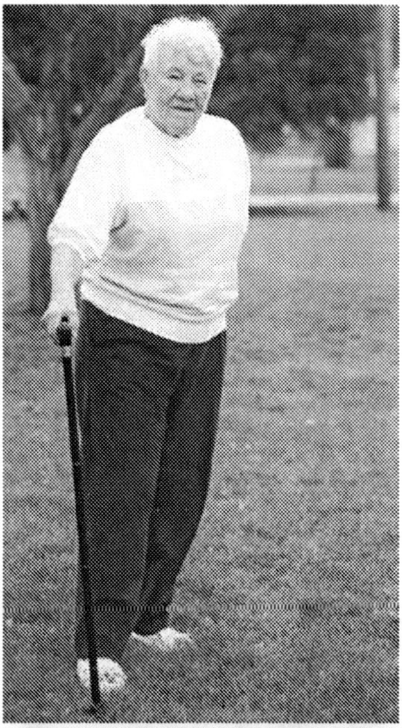
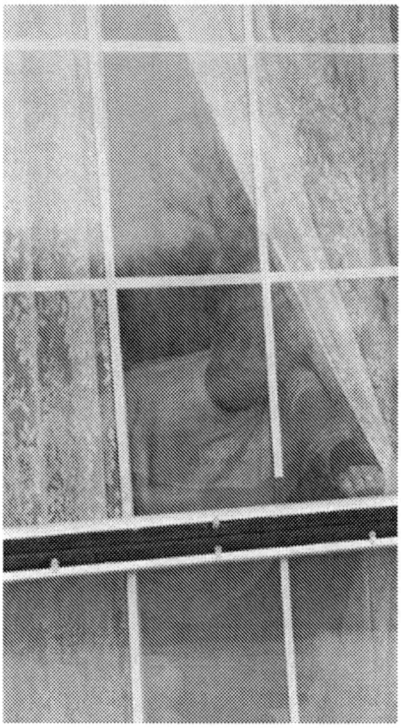
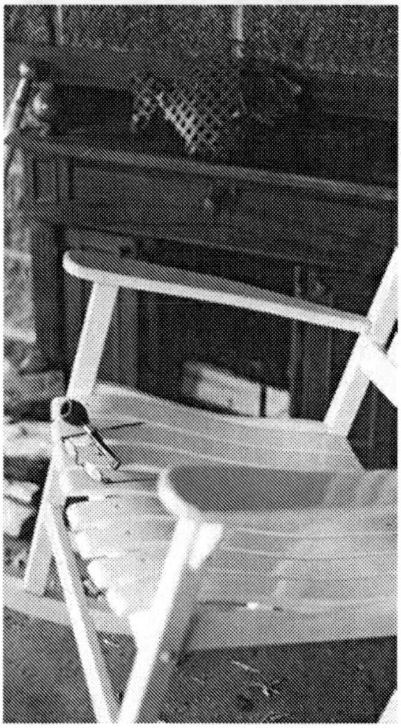

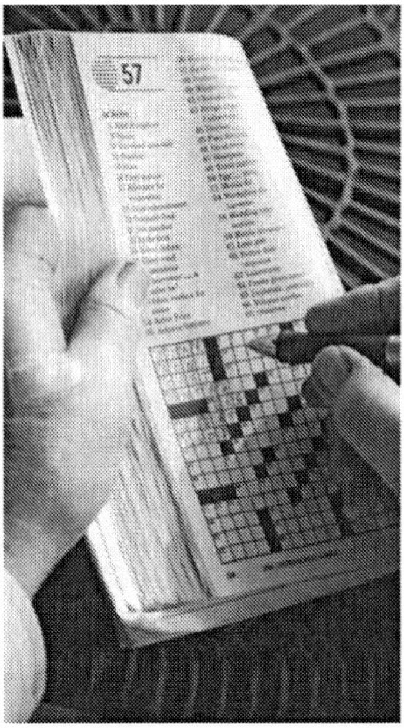
57

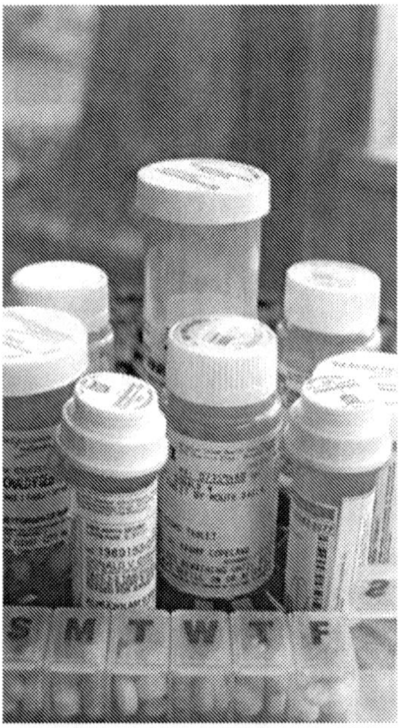
S M T W T F

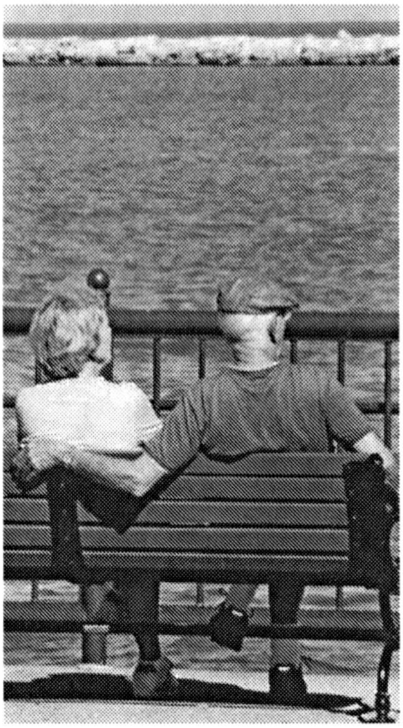

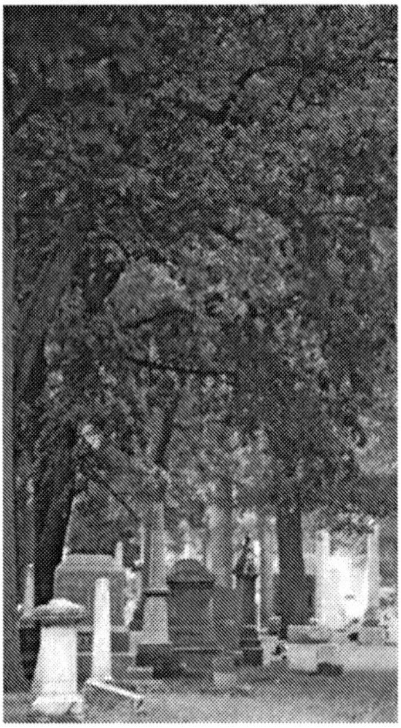

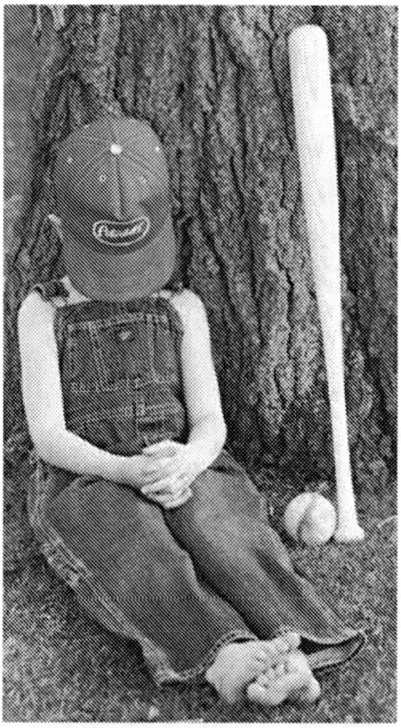

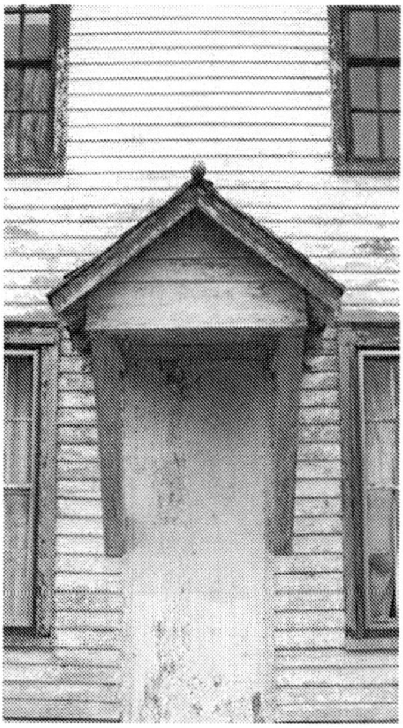

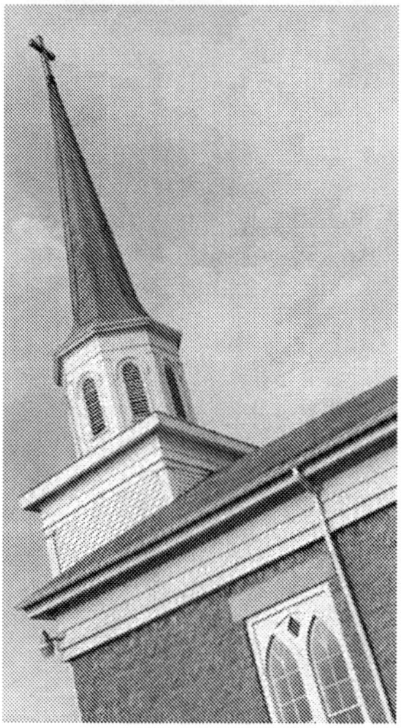

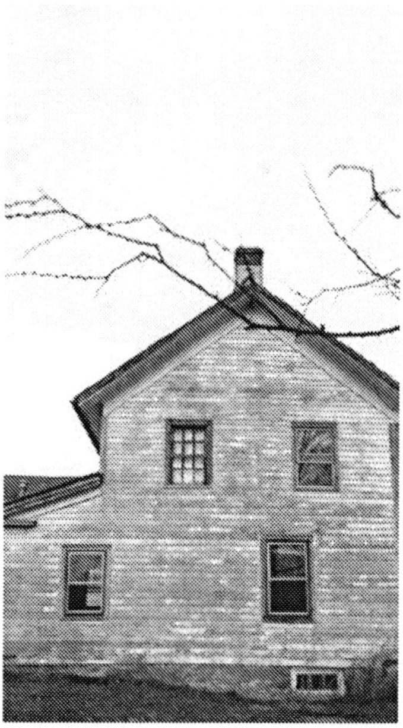

Guardian's Night Song

Sitting on the old gray porch
Feet upon the rail
Bouncing in the blue spring chair
When daylight starts to fail

Grandma joined me on the porch
Supper dishes washed and stacked
We hailed the neighbors walking by
On the sidewalk split and cracked

Church Street where the home place stood
Was lined with elms so tall
They touched mid street like dancers
Holding hands clear down a hall

Grandma wouldn't sit real long
It wasn't her routine
Back in the house she'd go fore long
Perhaps to cook or clean

I took time to wander
Round the yard, my nightly course
Surveying how the grass had grown
Followed bug trails to their source

Checked hydrangea for the wilt
Holly Hock, leaf minor trails
Mildew on the bee balm
The trees for sign of scales

But mostly I just wander
Breathing in the evening light
Assuring things were well
Wishing all the plants good night

Space Between My Ears

Did we really go to the moon? The answer's not so clear
Some say that it was just a ruse, they might be right I fear
The biggest fraud created for our cold-war-era fears
To stop the East from beating us in a space war lost by years

Why haven't we been going back since the initial flurry there?
Wouldn't it be better used than a space station in the air?
Wouldn't a glass biosphere which could support the human race
Be better than an aging station floating around the place?

Wouldn't a big telescope on the moon very firmly placed
Be better than the one we have wandering helplessly in space?
I would think our view of heaven would be made so much more clear
If we looked from the moon's perpetual night and not earths
atmosphere

Wouldn't it be much better and our glass of luck more full?
If we launched our explorer missions without earth's gravity pull?
The distance we could travel if we launched our ship from space
Would be proportionately further with the fuel we must now waste

Less heat less drag it all makes sense for reaching out beyond
Unless of course in reality we never left this pond
If the doubts we have are true and to the moon we did not go
It frightens me to think about the rest that we don't know

Superbowl Sunday

Religion as whole is a problem to mankind
Fed on human frailties in a search for the divine
Comfort in creation by a power just like us
Of course it has to look that way to minimize the fuss

Religion is like football or like soccer so it seems
Each one donning uniforms and picking up their teams
Competing for some coach who claims to know the real way
Victory's surely out of reach unless he has his say

You're not a real member unless you take one for the team
The best are really zealots who work up a head of steam
It doesn't matter who or what is sacrificed on the way
As long as their teams at the top on the final big game day

Technocrat

I finally got a cell phone though I've avoided it for years
I doubt that it is worth it except it eases my wife's fears
It never was a problem not so many years ago
If you weren't at home to catch the call, they'd have to let it go

With all the bells and buzzers they cram on that tiny phone
The only thing that I can do is get a dial tone
My fingers are too fat so if I want to push a number
I have to use a pencil to reach the key pad unencumbered

I cannot read the numbers popping up for my review
And even with my glasses on I must look a time or two
After that it's no surprise when the answer to my call
Is someone who doesn't know me and I don't know at all

Today I have to tell you that this phone may have to go
I was sitting in my office in my normal state of slow
When an officer came knocking with his hand upon his gun
Because this darned phone, by itself, had dialed 911.

I don't think a cell phone was called for in the human plan
Incessant talk was not required and belabors this old man
So many people use them to stay connected through the day
But when you're forced to listen, they've got nothing much to say

The Caning

I bought a cane at a craft fair several years ago
I didn't need it really it was just a thing for show
As I strolled around I noticed a few glances and a stare
They were trying to determine if my leg was really there

Not one to miss the opportunity to bathe in sympathy
I started limping around the show so everyone could see
First I limped upon my right leg then my left leg got the trick
Then I bent way over forward like my back had one bad crick

Imagination at this point began to run full bore
When a lady surely twice my age so kindly held the door
I began to dream up stories, as to how I got this case
And I added new dimension by showing pain upon my face

My theatrics rising quickly to the level of a star
I'm sure some people worried that they should help me to my car
I'm sure they thought I suffered from some horrible disease
Or even more, on some foreign shore, I left behind my knees

When I finally reached the car, I was chuckling, feeling smug
Then my wife got in the other side and gave me one big hug
She said that she was sorry that she missed me at the gate
And she wondered if I enjoyed myself and sorry she was late

She said a bunch of people milling around she heard complain
About some crazy faker acting up with some dumb cane
Some great big gal with tattoos whose name she learned was Sally
Was saying what she'd do to him if she caught him in an alley

"Why are you scrunching down like that?" my wife suddenly inquired
"Is your back hurting from walking around? You certainly looked tired?
I just knew that standing waiting for me caused your back to strain"
Then from her bags of purchases she presented me a cane

"I knew you wouldn't buy one for yourself you're not that kind
And I did one more thing for you and I hope that you don't mind
I asked the gal who makes them if she'd come over after lunch
She'll show you how to use it, her names Sally Ballsuncrunch."

My voice went up two octaves and I squeaked out," That was nice"
As I imagined scenes of a lesbian queen and my balls squeezed in a vice
Some tattooed female behemoth was soon to be at my door
Tipping the scales at a thousand pounds and eager to settle a score

I needed a plan for survival; clear the cobwebs that fill up my head
So when we reached home I reacted, and ran off to hide in the shed
Soon steps of doom at the entrance, signaled my fate at the door
But in stepped a meek little woman, she stood maybe four foot four

Relief on my face was apparent as I confidently drew up my frame
Reaching out with my hand in a welcome and politely asking her name
The slight little frame advanced to me, her little gray head at my vest
She said her name was Veda, and she reached with her hand to my chest

In an instant the stars almost doubled, I'm sure all the planets realigned
Bright little spots with black borders were swirling around in my mind
I've never before had a twister like the one she applied to my boob
On my knees in an instant to her level, at that point she called me a rube.

The rest of the message was garbled, due in part to the pressure and pain
Something about her sister Sally and what I could do with that cane
Emphasizing her wish that I remember, she gave one more painful twist
Just in case in my mind I had questions or points of her message I missed

The lesson I learned at that moment has followed me all through the years
Growing up is usually accomplished only after we've suffered some tears
Hopefully life's little lessons are worth all the memorable pains
I know as for me it is certain cuz my left boob still aches when it rains

Ol' Winky

I think I lost ol' Winky, he must have fallen off
I discovered he was missing yesterday while playing golf
I snuck off in the bushes to answer natures call
When I reached in to retrieve him there was nothing there at all

I suppose some guys were snickering at the loss of my dear friend
Some were laughing right out loud, my ego they'd offend
When my wife heard all about it, not the least was she contrite
She acted almost grateful and in her voice I sensed some spite

I went out to the garden where I like to contemplate
Joined by my dog named Doodles who I trust to commiserate
While Doodles started doodling just like Doodles likes to do
Digging deeply in my pocket for my balls I counted two

Ol' Winky wasn't in the place where he's usually put to rest
I remember how he hung there the first time he passed the test
The smile that over took me when I had him in my hand
Swinging back and forth so proudly, oh the feeling, it was grand

Without my old proud Winky, I'll be forced to give up the game
To try and play without him, well, it's really not the same
To have the drive and go the distance is only half the goal
'Cuz if you don't have your putter you'll just never reach the hole

The End of Cool

I was going through my closet as directed by my wife
To throw out all the memories accumulated in my life
Like the white belt with the matching shoes and heels four inches tall
I hid them back in seventy-three per my chiropractor's call

There were three shirts made of rayon which at the time were quite the rage
When you sweat they gave off an aroma like a gorilla in a cage
The top two buttons missing to reveal your manly hair
But it lost its magic passion because my chest was almost bare

The burgundy hip huggers with the legs cut in a flair
With the matching leisure jacket that for so long I could wear
I tried them on for memories sake but couldn't get them past my knees
My wife put them in a rag bag disregarding all my pleas

Bikini underwear in multicolor filled a box
I used to wear them daily with some matching rayon socks
My boys used to complain when I would slip them in a pair
And I bet they'd really whimper now that my belly's clear down there

I'm glad my wife is sensitive as I throw them in the bag
It only took two tissues to wipe her eyes from a laughing jag
No wonder I'm so slow to drain my life from memories pool
Each time I have to do this and witness the end of cool

The Life of Lucien

Lucien is so thin he disappears when turned sideways
An envious condition for a model now a day
But a real problem for him as a kid and not full grown
The other kids would tease him and would not leave him alone

All the torment changed remarkably when he'd reached the age of eight
When the other kids discovered he could reach through a sewer grate
Immediately a treasure, he received a real reprieve
Indispensable to everyone when their baseball he'd retrieve

In the summer kids played baseball in the middle of the block
Home plate was marked by someone's hat; first base a discarded sock
Second base was cardboard and third base a neighbor's tree
The batting team was the backstop, just in case the ball got free

Sometimes, they played softball, but they liked a hardball best
They chose up sides to square off, a kids hardest social test
If the teams didn't end up even as they often did not do
The last team would get Lucien and extra runs, well, they'd get two

Lucien was a dreamer and didn't really like the game
But he wanted to be with other kids, he hoped they felt the same
They would put him out in far right field just so they could say he played
But no one ever hit it there, an unspoken agreement made

Late in the second inning when a drive hit the third base tree
It shot across the street and hit poor Lucien in the knee
When Lucien pulled his pants leg up to look for damage done
The other team kept going, chalking up a huge home-run

His teammates were disgruntled and began to let off steam
They called Lucien a loser, he was ordered off the team
He sat down on the neighbor's porch joined by a friendly cat
He had to stay and watch because home plate was Lucien's hat

The cat seemed overly friendly and fixed Lucien with a stare
It would meow then run off quickly then return for another glare
Lucien finally followed the small cat in its excited state
It took him to the gutter and looked down the sewer grate

Lucien got down on his knee although it was plenty sore
He asked the frantic cat just what the heck it was looking for
Then deep down in the darkness of the grated sewer main
He heard the softest meowing from the bottom of the drain

He realized in an instant that a kitten was down there
With his skinny arm he reached and touched a little head of hair
Then gently by the scruff like the kittens mom is apt to do
He lifted out the kitten, then went back 'cuz there were two

The mother cat, relieved, gave Lucien's leg at least three rubs
Then two good head butts in the face as a thank-you from her cubs
Lucien smiled rewarded as the cat strolled down the street
Followed by the two penciled tails of kittens around her feet

Lucien hadn't noticed but the teams had stopped their play
Watching the small family as it wandered off that way
Then some one on his old team dusted off poor Lucien's hat
Then put his own down in its place and said "Lucien, it's you're bat"

The Writer

Fevered eyes bright and shining with anticipation
Tightened mouth pursed to expel the building stress
Stomach lurching, grabbing at itself
The bell tolling unanswered

Spinning vortex in the mind sea
Searching for the wind to move away
Harpoon poised to spear direction
Whaler becalmed on endless water

Blow damned wind of inspiration
Set this ship of mind to course
Cut the chains of deep sea anchors
Bite the lime with no grimace

Ink made from ashes of the dead
Tattoo scars record the past
Pierce the ear of recognition
Patch the eye to prepare for darkness

Map of mind holds no destination
Experienced only in where it has been
Redoubt against the tribulation
No tide rushes in to flush the thoughts

Vast sea of poisoned water
Creation spirit's parched tongue swelling
Voice strangled for lack of freshness
Washing my face with wasted tears

Dementia

Opened door through which I pass with body and mind memory
Each step stunting time backward until tomorrow disappears
Scent of your existence now gone, but still remaining somewhere near
Hidden under molding whiffs of old photographs

I strain to pull memory to my eyes, I cannot see you clearly
My mind searches through the thickness but is mired in forgetfulness
But I am aware of you, confusion embarrasses me
I know that I should know, I am aware of my growing short falls

Did I ask you? What did you answer? I should ask again
I cannot hold the words long against my memory
Like soap bubbles floating and breaking
As they land gently on my eyelashes, shields to recognition

I do not wish to strain your patience, why are you angry?
I hold no current events to feed the eager conversation
My participation flags into a state of idleness
Did I ask you? What did you answer? I should ask again

Why can't the memory return, what have I done wrong?
I should return to work, back to the normal
When did I stop working? How do you know and I don't?
Did I ask you? What did you answer? I should ask again

Desperation, untold frustration, being aware of being unaware
I cannot finish my thoughts,
The line falls off for a lack of the word which will not surface
Doors are closing closer behind me now

Did I ask you? What did you answer? I should ask again
I am not a child, why am I helpless?
Did I ask you? What did you answer? Should I ask you AGAIN?
I'm sorry I can't remember the question.

Weather-in-Law

I just can't wait for springtime
Winter's been an awful strain
It will be so refreshing
To complain about the rain

I'm pretty much exhausted
At a loss for a new bitch
With springtime soon approaching
Comes a conversation switch

I'll be able to regale them
With my thoughts about the mud
And what a problem life is
When you're dealing with the crud

Then summer sweeps upon us
With humidity and heat
And the pavement gives you third degree
When walking in bare feet

Then fall will come upon us
In a welcoming reprieve
Until you have to deal with
All the falling of the leaves

Of course we're back to winter
And we circle once again
It's amazing to me really
What a weather rut we're in

But I'm grateful for the seasons
Even though they all repeat
It gives me conversation
When the in-laws come to eat

World in a Match

Stoke the fire to build the heat
Cinders fall when burning's complete
Smoke rebelling up in great graying swirls
Escaping the fireplace, see how it twirls

Just sitting back in my rocker to gaze
A question I ponder as I view the haze
Is there creation in the smoke as it furls?
By starting this fire, did I start new worlds?

Comparing our world as I look out in space
To the flames and the smoke in my own fireplace
They seem so alike, their comparison strong
Perhaps creation's answer was here all along

The answers we search for in our outer space
Are answered quite clearly in my fireplace
The universe expanding, the planets, the stars
Galaxies swirling, and then dying in char

Time is man-made and is really not real
So distance, its measure, is irrelevant I feel
If we gathered the universe all up in one batch
It may not be bigger than the head of a match

I see all our being in those complex flames
But a lingering question unanswered remains
To complete this answer, there's just one small catch
Was it someone like me who first struck our match?

E-Male

Mary first told Margaret
Then Delores called up Jean
Who told her Jan had mentioned it
She's sure to tell Janine

Then Betty got the message
Which she passed to her friend Gwen
Who lives just down from Edith
In the condo on the end

Ann of course told Donna
Just exactly what was said
Then Glennis was informed
Even though she's sick in bed

Jackie heard from Peggy
Who told Becky at the mall
Who told her sister Jennie
Who'd suspected it since fall

When Clara told her husband
All the gossip that was spread
He told me that he heard her talk
But forgot just what she said

Evoligion

Ascended from some animal
How can we even try?
To claim we are a miracle
It's somewhat hard to buy.

I'm not offended believing
We came from something like an ape
Successfully surviving
Until we reached our present shape

In fact it's quite rewarding
To think our species started small
And with cunning and tenacity
Evolved into us all

What satisfaction is there?
If some celestial deity
Created us just as we are
To remain for eternity

No credit for the struggle
That it took to get us here
No hope that we grow better
By evolving year by year

Creationists and science
Theories all in a log jam
The only thing that matters
Is the truth that in fact"I AM"

Flower Power

One morning very early from my car I snuck some tools
To have them here in condo land is well beyond the rules
I tiptoed round the corner of my semi-owned estate
Determination surging for a garden I'd create

As quietly as possible I cut away some sod
I picked a spot right by the house where no one would have trod
A little space say two by four within which I could raise
Three pink petunias, a coral bell, and a daylily called "Daze"

I tried to dig with a garden trowel but it was so cheap it bent
The little shovel I tried next wouldn't even make a dent
It wasn't dirt in my small bed but sub soil construction clay
It was obvious this project would take more than just the day

I couldn't risk discovery by the condo committee clan
Whose job, though self appointed, was to judge each landscape plan
I had to accept the fact that this would take some major tools
No question I would run a foul of the clan and their phantom rules

Frustrated but tenacious and determined not to quit
I found I had the answer with an old time brace and bit
I drilled five holes into the clay it still was quite a fight
Then I pushed the plants down in the holes although the fit was tight

Retreating to my condo, content my mission was complete
I sat back in my rocker to take a load off of my feet
In less time than it takes for a cow pie to hit the floor
My happy thoughts were shattered by a knock upon my door

Of course it was the condo clan, the grand poobah old Ray.
Who claimed he had received complaints which must be fixed today
He claimed that someone passing and not snooping as I might think
Was offended by my garden, especially the color pink

I looked out of my door and no other person was about
I'm sure the real complainant was old Ray with his made up clout
He patrols the condo neighborhood morning, noon, and night
Like a little general who is always looking for a fight

I rolled my eyes and with a sigh gently pushed him out the door
I wasn't very pleasant and the truth is I was sore
That little condo Nazi was really getting out of hand
The time had come for me to rise and really take a stand

I fumed and fussed and railed against the injustice of the man
I contemplated impeachment with a scathing letter plan
I howled to my neighbors who insist they're on my side
It's not the plants per say but it's a matter of my pride

When the annual condo election day had finally rolled around
I was sure that fox in athletic socks would sure be run to ground
So I went out to the meeting, all the neighbors would be there
I rehearsed my speech repeatedly; I was loaded up for bear

Delivering my tome with a distinctive withering stare
Nominations for the officers were called on by the chair
Not a single neighbor said a thing or even raised a hand
Without a nomination then the committee they let stand

My neighbor is a widow and she looked about to cry
When gazing quickly at me she perceived my old stink eye
No one said a thing to me when I left which was just fine
Being so upset I could hardly sleep and was awake til almost nine

The next morning I descended on my little garden plot
I pulled up every flower and I stuck them in a pot
Today I got a letter from the old committee head
He said they had a problem because the pot I used was red!!!!!

Golly Wobbles

I noticed that just lately I've become a bit possessed
When ever I am standing up or bending to undress
I get the golly wobbles and it's really quite a scare
I usually sit back down or have to grab a chair

Sometimes the golly wobbles hit me when I'm looking up
I think I've really had them, since Doodles was a pup
It's just they seem more frequent then in past that I recall
I even got them yesterday while walking at the mall

I don't want to call the doctor and get my family all upset
So today when I take Doodles, I will ask my favorite vet
I'll pass it off on Doodles, the diagnosis will be free
And no one has to know the golly wobbles belong to me

Poor Doodles, poked and prodded, and an X-ray up his ass
Was finally released, but, with concern, they found a mass
The vet, he wasn't certain what the problem seemed to be
But he felt the golly wobbles was a symptom he might see

"By the way," the vet reflected as I slowly turned to go
"I wasn't going to say a thing but really you should know
I noticed when you came in and I'm sure it's no big deal
The shoes you're wearing on your feet are missing the right heel"

Doodles, glaring at me, as we made our way back home
I knew he felt repayment was deserved with extra bones
The next day the heel resurfaced, it was lying in the grass
Obviously, the reason behind Doodles unknown mass

Not surprisingly my golly wobbles have started to abate
Since having my old shoe reheeled, I started feeling great
But my wife found out about it, now my walk has lost its strut
I'm scheduled to have my doctor take an X-ray up my butt

Hair in the Ear

Don't forget to kick some ass!
What? I asked somewhat in shock
DON"T FORGET TO GET SOME GAS!
Oh, of course and turned the lock

At the store get tan and greens!
Huh? What was that? I couldn't tell
AT THE STORE GET TANGERINES!
Crying out loud, you don't have to yell

I don't know what's wrong with some people today
They can't seem to talk in the usual way
They all seem to mumble and speak in some code
An obvious sign of a mind overload

I think there's a spark in my space underwear!
Oh cripes what a vision would you please repeat?
I THINK THERE"S A PARKING SPACE RIGHT OVER THERE!
I think it is best if I park in the street

While I do the shopping mop the front of aisle four!
I think should I have too? Are they unemployed?
WHY ARE'NT YOU STANDING OUT FRONT BY THE DOOR?
I do what you tell me and now you're annoyed!

People no longer can pronunciate
They should learn to speak clearly before it's too late
Tonight for example, what does my wife mean?
She rolled over and kissed me and said HAVE STREET JEANS

Hell's Little Angel

OH No! There goes Lucille
I bet she's headed for the mall
I hate to see her driving
She's only four feet tall

At 90 years old she drives slowly
I'm afraid at her age that she'll crash
She sees out the window by squinting
Between the steering wheel and the car's dash

She sits so low it's amazing
She's maybe two feet off the floor
Two small hands at two and ten
And her shawl caught in the door

When she creeps down to the corner
Her car will start to stall
It's an old standard transmission
Never uses the clutch at all

She puts the car in neutral
Revs the engine up a bit
Then slams the car in first gear
I'm surprised she's not been hit

Lurching into the intersection
Her signal blinking for a right
She turns left into traffic
I close my eyes in fright

A trucker brakes his big rig
Gives his air horn one loud toot
Lucille rolled down her window
And gives him a finger salute

I'm really glad it's winter
From her mouth I see a blue fog
I hate to think what could have happened
In summer when she's riding her hog

Isolation Ward

Perhaps our planets just a step
In a development well planned
This earth where we will all be kept
So we don't get out of hand

We know that we are distant
From the universal core
Perhaps put here in an instant
As an isolation ward

Our eventual resolution
To gain a perfected mind
Requires cruel evolution
Consuming all living kind

Our carbon based existence
A body furnace you might say
Much stronger than our resistance
Requires stoking every day

We're required to take from the living
Whether flesh or plants and their seed
It's a world of taking not giving
Not a shared universal need

But our ultimate independence
Won't require that we must eat
This pupated state of transcendence
Through death all life defeats

Released from this planet prison
Life for life, no longer the cost
Separation will end, no division
And return from the land of the lost

The true source to which we'll have ascended
When the transitions effectively made
Will disclose how the universe was defended
And isolation the price that was paid

Just a Little Support

I found a hole in my pants just as I got to work
I hate when that happens 'cuz I feel like such a jerk
Walking round in the office with my rear end taking air
I would change them if I could, but I don't have an extra pair

Of course, there was the giggling and the can't-believe-it stare
And the people who would point it out as if I weren't aware
The chucklehead next to my desk, who's life's not worth a think
Reached up and pinched my butt while I was washing in the sink

I don't suppose the hole was what had really got them going
I think it was my choice of underwear that now was showing
While dressing in the dark I put the first pair on I found
They were really tight, but lately, I've put on some extra pounds

I thought they were some jockeys which I very seldom wear
But instead they were pink maternity pants my wife had stored in there
So all day long I took the razz from all the office crew
But, I swear, I'll hit the next smart guy who asks me when I'm due

Life's Reflection

Looking at the paper after Sunday morning brunch
That's the meal I usually eat between my breakfast and my lunch
I routinely check the obits, a habit normal to my age
Relieved I don't know anyone, I turn to the anniversary page

The pictures make me chuckle when they show before and now
Some couples married sixty years you've got to wonder how
The looks they have upon their faces suggest a lot of strain
I wonder which one was the cause of all the wedded pain

Others are truly happy with the situation they've been in
You can tell which ones they are by their smiling open grin
The other thing about them is they both now look the same
Melded both together in much more than just a name

I wonder looking at them if living to one hundred and three
Then taking a picture of them would one face be all I see
So intoned with each other that they both just sing one note
Their lives so intertwined their differences now remote

I take my wife out to the hallway; tuck her head under my chin
And look into the mirror, compare the faces seen within
I guess I have to tell you that it won't take 'til one hundred and three
Though two heads were in the mirror, only one face looked at me

Memorial Revenge

I've decided when I die, please no monument of stone
I don't want to be interred in just one grave site all alone
I'd like to find an expert in the field of botany
To convert me into a noxious weed and name it after me

I think it would be fitting in my final state of grace
To be scattered all around and just to pop up every place
To be a total scourge of my neighbor's pristine lawn
A reminder every summer that old Dan is never gone

Resistant to all poisons I suppose that I should be
And give a rash to people when they try to tread on me
I would like to smell of chicken when it's left out in the heat
Or perhaps like grungy sweat socks just pulled off some dirty feet

I'd be resistant to the weather so I'd grow from shore to shore
But I'd like to be nutritious if I'm eaten by the poor
My roots would break up concrete at the local big box store
My reputation would be the subject of all future gardening lore

Creeping Charley and the Kudzu would be all a friend to me
But would pale in comparison to the problem I would be
Dandelions and wild parsnip, instead of me, would be a lift
Confusion and profusion, my environmental gift

I know it wouldn't happen, but it's fun to sit and dream
Blowing off the small frustrations and the odd-head full of steam
But just maybe, in the future some old gardener, hat in hand
Will tell you he can't save your lawn because it's full of Dan.

Might I Suggest

One thing I could tell the young and some value they might find
Is always have an option when you're making up your mind
Don't ever put yourself into a place with just one door
Make sure you have an exit just in case your choice was poor

If looking at a problem or an opportunity
With horizons that are way too high or too far off to see
Be sure you have an exit before you start to go
Usually, that exit is the chance to just say no

If you could lose the chance to just simply walk away
By crossing some enticing bridge you're afraid that would not stay
If there's pressure at the moment, a rush to decide your present fate
Don't worry, good things reappear, I suggest you're best to wait

Waiting is the hardest thing you'll do throughout your life
It's never easy when you feel you need to change some strife
Change will come regardless, but only in due course
Mistakes are made most often when we make a change by force

Miser Magnet

I would like to be a miser, with a hidden stack of gold
I've decided that is what I'll be when I reach the state of old
I'll hoard each dollar that I get and count them one,two,three
Of course it's not as easy as it really ought to be

First I started hiding all my change in a worn-out coffee can
But I had to cash it all in just to pay my insurance plan
Then I hid a dollar in my drawer in some old athletic jocks
But my wife found it and spent it to replace my worn out socks

I got two dollars from a rebate for a special at the store
But I had to give it to the kids that were collecting for the poor
So I bought a metal detector, I'd get rich from things that were lost
But so far I've only found enough to cover its shipping cost

I did learn a real lesson when I dug up a power line
The shock I got was nothing compared to the cost of replacement fine
So my plan to be a miser has begun to lose its lure
Just what I'll be when I get old, I'm really not that sure

I took one more shot at it when I put some in the bank
They gave me a small toaster as a symbol of their thanks
But when the first statement came, they kindly asked me please
If I'd wish to send it back or send ten bucks to cover fees

It's obvious that my destiny is still up in the air
At this point in my life I've started really not to care
I must take some time and truly re-evaluate my goals
As for a money magnet I've been cursed with two south poles

Steak in the Heart

I had a friend named Alex who had gone on a great cruise
When I asked him how he liked it he rolled his eyes and said,"
Bad news"
He complained about the food although the quality was great
He had ordered a small steak and half the cow was on his plate

I couldn't understand why he complained. Was he for real?
To never cruise again because of the sizes of his meal
I suppose that Alex really was a product of his past
When meals were not a given, not to waste, and made to last

I notice older people complain about the portion and its size
They get full on garnish, half a sandwich and three fries
It's true I like to eat just like other gray hairs do at four
But I still eat biggy portions and if allowed I'd go for more

Thinking of my friend, his perspective gives me pause
He really made a point; there was merit to his cause
We really eat too much, never think about the waste
In fact we cram it down so fast we've lost the sense of taste

Alex passed away a short time after my own Dad
I miss them both immensely and the great times that we all had
I try to think about them when I sit down to a meal
Remembering Alex and my Dad with the fullness that I feel

I'm grateful for the portions of each one, Alex and Dad
Each portion that they fed me from their lives I'm truly glad
Although they both have left me, in my life they're a big part
Their memories held in place by Alex's steak stuck in my heart

Only True Fact

Who, Who, Who
Every one we know
What, What, What
Eventually will go
Where, Where, Where
Perhaps to an afterglow
When, When, When
As life's river stops its flow
Why, Why, Why
We can no longer grow
How, How, How
To each a different ending show

Passing Gas

Did you ever notice how we concern ourselves with gas?
I mean the price paid at the pump not the kind that we all pass
Each time I drive my relations around it's like they're keeping score
Announcing, as we pass each place, what a gallon of gas sells for

Another thing that irks me is the pricing with a point
What if you want one gallon when you pull into the joint
It says right out in open that it's two-twenty-nine point nine
But when you pay the man he wants two-thirty by design

Think about it for a moment for each ten gallons that they make
You pay an extra penny for the gas you're forced to take
If you multiply that penny by the millions of gallons sold
The amount they get from extra sales is a staggering pot of gold

Of course they say you pay just for the gallons that you take
But you can't buy just one gallon, because a penny they can't break
So you're forced to take some extra even though you don't want more
Imagine how much extra gas is sold from shore to shore

To conserve the world's resources at one-third ounce per each gallon
And stop from splitting pennies will remain I'm sure a challenge
But who draws benefit from the trickle, that's the hitch
It's neither you nor I, that in the end, are getting rich

The point is that a gallon of gas should be an even cent
To stop the extra usage by design we could prevent
I think it gives new meaning though I think it rather crass
Oil companies should be cited, if we catch them passing gas

Only Once Around

Pills always popping
Blood pressure dropping
Or rising, neither is good

Vision is failing
Often times ailing
Can't enjoy life as we should

Breathing is shallow
Skin looks like tallow
Back of our heels are like wood

Watch for tomorrow
How many will follow
Would we go back if we could?

Too many miles
Although there were smiles
It's doubtful if we really would

Memory Medallions

I have seventeen medallions on a little Christmas tree
They represent the dogs and cats that spent some time with me
Each one is just a memory now since death has made its call
I cherish every moment that I got to spend with all

Most of them were strays or from the humane society
I seldom knew their lineage; it didn't mean a thing to me
Each was a special being, walking with me on life's track
Their places would be ready if some how they could come back

I hope that I was kind enough and they were happy as a result
They seemed to like me anyway regardless of my faults
I've heard a little saying that would sure apply to me
If dogs don't go to heaven, then send me where they'll be

Passing time remembering each soft and loving face
Comic personalities, each with their strength and grace
I'm sure that in the years to come more medallions there will be
Until the last medallion, which is mine, hangs on the tree

Man of Men

Why can Jesus not just be a man?
Who loved a wife, had children, and planned
Why must his life be devoid of the joy?
Seeing his face in his child, girl or boy

Why can't religions in their present state
Define him as someone to whom we relate
What's wrong with admitting he may have been blessed?
At Canaan the bridegroom and not just a guest

His perfection lay not with his physical form
What if it were found he'd been naturally born?
Would that make his message unworthy to hear?
Or were miracles needed to perk up our ear?

Would it be horrific if we found his remains?
I think it would diminish resistance and strains
It's not in the man but the message he gave
That transcended death and arose from the grave

The message, the message, the message it hosts
A trinity of one, first son, father, then ghost
Procession of life from our birth to our death
The only real miracle is in our first breath

Our mission is simple, to be honest and just
To love fellow men as ourselves is a must
Embrace his teaching and follow that plan
Then Jesus could be just a regular man

I don't need miracles to validate worth
I think it's a plus if he came from this earth
No need to argue or the church to defend
Christ, as he was, a man of all men

Security Blanket

All the answers we are seeking exist in plain view
Clouded away from our eyes only by our own insistence
Desires formed from misconceptions long ago borne

Truths swirling in transparent clouds
Awaiting our willingness to be molded into reality
Startling, shocking, blinding in their obviousness

The light of realization itself is misconstrued
We find no comfort in its brilliance
Heaven is our conclusion

Disturbed by strangeness that does not reflect our face
Possibilities of the true reality rejected as distorted
Unable to fit in the mold man's mind has created

Perpetuity is a child's blanket we hold
Comfort received from its being held in our minds
Death has no memory

Under Achiever

In the life of an under achiever
The title to which I belong
Like a baseball pitching reliever
You can rely on me but not too long

I'll be there in a heart beat to help you
For a moment I'll give you my all
But longevity isn't my strong point
So let's not pretend I won't fall

My attention span is quite deficient
But when it's in gear it's quite clear
My mouth and my ear aren't connected
So please don't believe all you hear

Don't fret when I rise to a challenge
And seem like I've mastered the call
I don't have the needed resilience
To continue to dribble the ball

Like writing this poem with its rhyming
And retaining the meter and time
I'm getting fatigued with the tempo
So forget it

Epitaph

I would like to tell you something
It would really make you shout
If I could just remember
What the subject was about

It had something to do with living
No, perhaps that's not quite true
I think it was forgiving
No, that's really not the view

Was it something that I heard?
Perhaps it's something that I said
This is going to drive me crazy
'Cuz it's buzzing in my head

I don't think it really matters
In the long run you'll find out
If it's really that important
Someone else will give a shout

If you're reading this one evening
In the evening obits spread
That's it I just remembered
Yesterday they found me dead

Crying for Remembrance

As the tree grows
The branches expand
Each reaching out
As far as it can

The bottom grows wider
The top not quite so
Nature controls
A direction to go

The youthful top dances
The sun helps it grow
But shadows are cast
On its elders below

In shadow the old ones
Survive but grow dark
Knurled and woody
Brittle and stark

Just like those old ones
Who give up their space
We help lift our youth
Without sun on our face

So I relate
To my own family tree
For those who are here
Or in future will be

When you feel
The sun on your face
Remember the branch
That I held up in place

An Ending

Gray and cold like winter holding its sterile sheet over its head
Stainless steel clouds weigh down the spirit's rising
Unpulsing cold knots end the cramping palsy
Hands wobbling outstretched like a mop heads on a much too thin handles

Pools of black encircle chalky film covered eyes
The throaty rattle stops, foam creeping slowly from distorted lips
Life sounds ceasing, replaced by screeching gurney wheels
The empty cocoon waits in the hall for filing.

No more heat will flow from the burned out furnace
The fuel of emotions has run out
All feeling evaporated to dry dust
Complete acceptance is all that remains

Winter Screams

The frozen door like a screaming child torn from its mother
Resists the desperate effort to open
Warm smells escaping in mass through the crack
Spring insistent, winter fighting to remain

Softness arising with afternoon sun
Cold water droplets thrown onto a bright new fire
Winter striving to staunch the warmth
Ice reclaiming earth at moon rise

Winter hardness enveloped in the soft blanket of its enemy
Attempting to throw off the closeness
Longing for the sharpness of frosted breath
Both joined as the battle ebbs and flows

Spring sun driving back the cold edges
Ice soldiers throw off their armor and run to hiding
Seeking darkness as shelter
Winter's insurgency waits to return

Neither army claims complete victory
Each holding sway for a short time
Territory claimed only to be recaptured
Scars of war, worn only by the gentle earth watching

Veneration

When I was young I would have written of love
Physical longing, excitement in deceit
Carnal hunger licking and penetrating
Wetness slipping between us

With age I write of warmth and bonding
Caresses met with smiles and comfort
Tender moments without words
Shared thoughts requiring no verbal reply

Transcending into the true love
Bonding emotion in constant consideration
For the other half of my brain
I knew of you before I knew who you were

The Passing

Approach me very carefully, baggy pants and crooked hat
I may not hold the strength you posture but I am dangerous
Don't encroach upon the air space ringing my aging self
Unspoken buffer to be breached by only the familiar

I sense your closure, shuffling melodic steps
I see your posture sulking and dragging of the foot
Brought forward only by the strength of a thrown hand
Body dipping sign of pride from a world not my own

I would accept you if I understood your view of truth
But my questions, I fear, will only be met with laughter and mocking
Is it your own discomfort in my approach that would bring this rebuff?
The only thing we currently share

Passing now, looking away, like dogs afraid to catch the eye
Tension throwing a magnetic thrust of two south poles
Bouncing off each others redoubt of mistrust
Curiosity catching us as we both look back

Gramma Donna

My mother just turned eighty at the beginning of this year
Most people at that age would just be grateful to be here
But mom is still a mover and a shaker in high gear
More energy than sense perhaps a calamity is near

She crawls out on her roof to wash a windowed second floor
I caught her moving rocks that weighed two hundred pounds or more
To cut an old dead branch I think she might have climbed a tree
It's scary to hear the things she's done although she won't tell me

She has some aches and pains that I suspect should slow her down
But you'd hardly recognize it by the way she runs around
She has to go shopping almost every single day
What most of us call work is just her normal day of play

She moved into a condo so that she wouldn't have the chores
Related to the yard work and the things you do out doors
But for two years she's been planting an expanding landscape plan
Pouring concrete, building fences, enough work for three grown men

She made me help her purchase a step ladder ten feet tall
So she could change the light bulbs in the living room and hall
I told her I would do it if she'd simply give a call
But I think it makes her feel less old if she can do it all

Today she asked me for some help to start up her chainsaw
Will this be another specter that we now call shock and awe?
As long as she is happy running here and running there
But it's better if I can watch her from my worn out rocking chair

Spring in My Strep

Taking a spring walk and breathe in the air
Letting the spring breezes blow through my hair
I look at the sun and then wait for a sneeze
Now I remember the pain in my knees

My eyes start to itch and then water and run
My temperature registers one hundred and one
My throat starts to feel like an old gravel road
My voice sounds as though I have swallowed a toad

Winter itch is gone now but replaced with a rash
My taste buds are shot, food tastes like old sour mash
My sinuses swelling I can't smell a thing
The pressures so great that it makes my ears ring

Those newest spring flowers so pretty at first sight
Are flinging their pollen which now I must fight
Decongestants and antihistamines win a place by my bed
But they make me so tired I can't lift up my head

The season of awakening can fill me with dread
When the sweet smelling plants wake my allergies instead
People get giddy with Miss Spring when they see her
But I just come down with a case of spring fever

Hellth

Gertrude has some bone spurs so she walks upon her toes
Burt has sinusitis so he always blows his nose
Barney's heavy smoking has resulted in a hack
While Bridget's double D's have caused a problem in her back

Orin wears two socks to help the rash between his toes
Ernie has a truss but if it helps just heaven knows
Ethyl wears support hose for her varicosed blue veins
Winston wears a knee brace to protect it from the strains

Robert has two hearing aides although they're not much good
Gerald's new prosthesis has improved since it's not wood
Jeff's colostomy is better since he got the brand new drain
Vicky's medication helps contain that wandering pain

Winny's wandering eye with the new patch has settled down
Vincent's facial scars have turned a brand new state of brown
Pete gave up his crutches for a deluxe electric cart
Wendall has a pacemaker with self sensing auto start

Last night we got together to observe our friend Clyde's wake
While those of us who could were given juice and chocolate cake
Warren turned his voice box up and toasted all our wealth
At having such good friends and thanking God for our good health

Home Again

Wandering through my gardens I was somewhat taken aback
I should have been more diligent last fall and that's a fact
I forgot to put some pots away, honey suckle needs a trim
Wisteria is so large that instead of branches it's got limbs

Half the roses were not covered I suppose they won't come back
The patio is really dirty and it has a brand new crack
The cattails in the pond are spewing gobs of fluffy seeds
That's all I need this summer is a bunch more cattail reeds

I found my pruning scissors stuck by rust to my back wall
I must have wandered off and just forgot them there last fall
My garden wagon served as a latrine for all the cats
That's better than the year before when one had used my hat

My garden sheds so cluttered you can hardly get inside
It used to be so organized I would show it off with pride
Dried and withered bulbs now putrefy on the back shelf
It smells so strong of cat pee I'm embarrassed for myself

Most of the tools are rusty because they sat against the floor
In water from the melting snow that had blown in through the door
Fertilizer sat in bags that now were more like blocks
Seed packs melted on the floor I think that they were phlox

One thing caught my eye it was my favorite rocking chair
Waiting by the fireplace all soot filled from lack of care
It felt good to be back in my favorite dreaming place
Although it was a mess it put a smile upon my face

Voyeur

Watching the clock
Watching the weather
Watching my speed
Observing a feather

Watching my words
Watching her face
Watching my checkbook
Looking for space

Watching my neighbors
Watching the lawn
Watching the children
See when their gone

Watching the left
Watching the right
Watching for signs
Beholding the light

Watching an opening
Watching the door
Watch for the day
When I'll need watch no more

Want

Want goes beyond what we all really need
It gives birth to anger and stimulates greed
It propagates envy, avarice, and hate
It makes us put more than we need on our plate

Want, once you have it, can never be filled
It's the one driving force for which people are killed
Want for more land, want for a name
Want to be known, fifteen minutes of fame

Because of want we'll be bought with a coin
Sacrifice children for a group that we join
Give up our souls for a perceived better plan
Want is the seed of religion in man

Want to ascend beyond what we have here
Willing to murder for a future unclear
Convinced that our wanting is condoned by our God
Supporting a crusade or religious jihad

The God that exists whether Christian or Jew
Islamic, or Buddhist to name just a few
When refined to pure light and man's wants are defamed
One God will most likely be all that remained

Life in a Bubble

If time as we know it was hard to define
And bent in a circle and not a straight line
Instead of a dimple in the fabric of space
What if it was round and returned to its place

What if there was more than our one universe
Where ever they touch a black hole soon would burst
Some larger, some smaller from each other they draw
By vacuum they suck like the end of a straw

The edge of our universe might be really thin
Black holes more like pores that we find in our skin
Each universe round side by side they all sit
Like bubbles they mold to each other to fit

So it's possible that what we see as our home
Is perhaps not so solid and simply soap foam

Rubber Dollar

I only have a dollar to buy my lunch for the whole week
I guess I have to say my budget needs a certain tweak
I suppose it would be better if I missed a couple meals
It would be a simple lesson as to how the hungry feel

The first day wasn't bad; I found some cookies in a drawer
The second day was better there was cake I'm fifty-four
The third day a business brunch catered by a customer
Three days without a lunch is really tough and that's for sure

The fourth day there was pizza brought in by the guys downstairs
Two of them won't eat it so of course I must eat theirs
On Fridays there are donuts and a buffet from the staff
Topped off with six deserts and a latte filled carafe

As I left that afternoon there's a vendor by the door
Who told me I looked peckish; I had to tell him I was poor
He handed me two dogs with cheese and kraut and a bag of chips
I offered him the dollar, "Some other time," he gently quips

I had to see the doctor for my annual review
He brought up several issues, the concerns he felt were two
He claimed that I had gained some weight that I could not afford
And my cholesterol was high; I have to tell you I was floored

It's a mistake I'm certain a second opinion I must seek
I told him how I only had a buck for lunch all week
I've hardly eaten anything because I've been so strapped
In fact I've felt so weak because starvation has me sapped

I bought a candy bar for energy to get me home
I had a large soda that I'm sure was mostly foam
My wife told me when I got home that I was looking weak
She knows I only had a buck for lunch to last the week

Night Raider

I sneak off to the kitchen; it's the seventh time tonight
I open up the fridge and I try to hide the light
Perhaps there's something in there that I missed the times before
I re-search all the shelves; check out the freezer and the door

I mentally reflect if there's a specific food in mind
Though I'm really not that picky, I'd eat anything I find
Do I want something salty or do I want something sweet
I'll probably pick both so it's a balanced late night treat

All the new leftovers from tonight have disappeared
The choices have diminished since I've checked six times, I feared
I settle for sour pickles and the last piece of a pie
A handful of green olives and baked beans, it's worth a try

While I am gently grazing, taking in all the food groups
A hunk of cheese, a swig of milk, and a bowl of Sugar Loops
My wife slips up behind me, then shrieks at me," Dan good Lord!"
"You can't be really hungry; I suggest that you're just bored"

She forces closed the fridge door and she makes me go to bed
But I can't go to sleep because of thoughts now in my head
Had I missed that special something perhaps it was hidden in a drawer
I knew I had to get up one more time and check for sure

As soon as her gentle snoring told me she had gone to sleep
I slipped back out of bed, for mission eight I had to keep
But when I took a step her gentle snoring kind of stopped
So I quickly changed from tip toe to a high kneed kind of hop

This morning when I woke my wife was nowhere to be seen
I heard the dishwasher going and she called out kind of mean
"Did you go in this fridge?" I answered back a curt," No Maam"
Then she caught me scraping, from my face, some old dried up peach jam

The Pontificate

Fall from grace
To inner space
Why can't it ever be outer?

Weak retort
Requires we abort
It usually goes to the shouter

Threats to remember
If you're not a member
There's no chance that you will be saved

Not really your choice
They say you've no voice
It's a matter of how you behaved

Race to the tomb
Before there's no room
Just special souls are protected?

Heavens no race
Stay here in place
Enjoy life, you'll not be rejected

Daylight Slaving Time

I have to wonder why they have to mess with the spring clock
Jumping out ahead has always put me into shock
It doesn't matter if they give you Sunday to adjust
My body seems to need at least a week and that's a must

My poor cat Grady isn't good at adjusting to the plan
Neither is my dog, named Jet, or the remainder of my clan
We're back to waking in the dark, we had just escaped that scene
It was getting light when I got up, to push ahead is just plain mean

It doesn't seem to make much sense any more that I can see
Like the Electoral College or a black and white TV
Or a flashbulb for a camera, a radio with just two knobs
A cartridge fountain pen or pipes made from old brown corn cobs

A vinyl set of records, Beta or a VCR
A book of S&H green stamps that I'd get when I gassed my car
My 64 K computer, the salesman told me would last for life
Platform shoes, bell bottoms, or the fur coat for my wife

Daylight savings time without much effort lost its charm
When whoever claimed we needed it laid the blame on some poor farm
There always seems to be a reason as to why things go away
So my reason is the fact it sucks, stop messing with my day

Don't Diddle with the Middle

Without middle you have no top
Top goes to bottom without any stop
Top needs middle to keep bottom away
Bottom does the work while top likes to play

Bottom has muscle and accused of no brains
While top uses favors and political games
Middle has mass and substance it seems
Cementing together the two other extremes

If middle is weakened with too many on top
Society tumbles and comes to a stop
Everything top does is made out of air
And only has substance if middle is there

Bottom has strength but cannot really talk
It needs middle to translate so that it can walk
Bottom is sweat and requires middle's care
It will dry out and die if exposed to top's air

Top as the head in a mirror it's seen
Applauding itself with inflated esteem
Bottom complains though it had a good chance
Life's dues it refused now it just can't advance

Societal figure with both head and feet
Without middle's body would not be complete
Top's head, bottom's feet must be kept well apart
They both need middle's stomach, two lungs and its heart

Social Mirage

Sitting on the outside of a heady social ring
Looking at the consequences I don't miss a thing
Obligations are the cost I'm not obliged to pay
I'm happy not to have to live my life in such a way

Constant worry that you might by some blundering oversight
Offend someone you hardly know by words they take as slight
Belonging to the club can be a weight around your neck
Financially a burden but a must I do suspect

All the posturing and posing just to say that you belong
Connections for advancement not real friendship all along
Shallow people acting as if they somehow really care
If opportunity is absent then you're best to not be there

If they think that you have money or a social inside track
They'll give you recognition but they hope to get some back
They are always looking for a chance to collect some hidden fee
When they honor you with presents or a fake college degree

I want to acknowledge all the people without fame
Just the average people that pass by without a name
The high and mighty need you for without you they must pause
Unable to sharpen their mirage of social claws

Parent Projects

My son created a science project for the school last week
He worked upon it weekends until he smoothed out every tweak
He studied the computer for a factual report
He even asked me questions just in case, a last resort

The day arrived to show it, so he borrowed my old truck
To haul it to the school and set it up, I wished him luck
That night at the science fair I over heard him say
How happy he'd become because his daughter got an "A."

Next year I'm pretty certain he will have to make a car
I think the pinewood derby is the next one up so far
Perhaps a diorama made from newspaper and flour paste
With Indians and Cowboys riding horses aptly placed

Children don't be sad because you can't participate
I guarantee you'll have your chance, but for now you'll have to wait
When you grow up and have some kids according to the plan
You too will get to do school projects done by your old man

Grandpa-pular

Old Jake had a tooth that he could stick out just for fun
We kids would flock around him and try to see how it was done
When he would open up his mouth the tooth was no longer there
But when we turned around the tooth would magically appear

Ol' Billy has a thumb we were sure he could pull apart
He also had a finger that if you pulled would make him fart
Grandpa Al could make a cloud of smoke come out his ear
And cast a spell on warts so they'd be gone within the year

Grandpa Jessie's missing finger gave us all a thrill
And the how he lost it story of the hole in the windmill
How his mother sewed it up with a needle and some thread
Put his finger in a flowerpot, then went to bake some bread

Now I am a grandpa and I hope I have some luck
And get my grandchild laughing when I talk like Donald Duck
Their eyes fill with amazement when they're in their tender years
When they're laughing at their grandpa then there's no more time
for tears

The Patriots

Hurray it's now summer, the fourth of July
It's ninety-five out, not a cloud in the sky
I've waited for this now we're half through the year
In less than six months Christmas carols we'll hear

The sun is a scorcher; it burned Pat's bald head
I'm sure it is sore and it really turned red
Tom wore a cap now his forehead is white
In fact it's so bad that it glows in the night

I, on the other hand, had a hat too
But I sweat so profusely it dyed my head blue
So on this occasion while our wives tongues all wag
We sit at the picnic, an American flag

Cycle of Circles

Waiting births wishing
Wishing births dreaming
Dreaming births anguish
Anguish births scheming

Scheming births lying
Lying births pain
Pain births change
Change births gain

Gain births envy
Envy births hating
Hating births action
Action births waiting

Politics

Regulations
Paid persuasions
Exemptions bought
John Q caught

Push out the poor
Bar the door
Elite know best
Forget the rest

Oil companies toying
World destroying
Interests spying
Politics lying

God in dollars
Guessing scholars
Can't be wrong
Same old song

Walking Away

Looking down the railroad tracks
You could wander alone for miles
Leave all the troubles far behind
Walk away from all life's trials

Walk away from obligations
Walk away from bad times you've had
Walk away from all commitments
Walk away from thoughts that are sad

Walk away from disappointment
Walk away from people you hate
Walk away from the poor and the helpless
Walk away from your own children's fate

Walk away from expectations
Walk away from prying eyes
Walk away from other's resentment
Walk away from your lover's sighs

No matter how far you keep walking
There are always more cares on the shelf
Requiring that you keep on walking
Because you can't walk away from yourself